A Busy Day

CONTENTS

NATIONAL GEOGRAPHIC

Hampton-Brown

School Publishing

Sounds for <u>b</u>, <u>w</u>, <u>j</u>, <u>z</u>

Look at each picture. Read the words.

Example:

<u>b</u>ag

<u>**w**</u>ag

<u>j</u>am

<u>z</u>ig <u>z</u>ag

High Frequency Words
day
from
good
she
us
very

Key Words

Look at the picture. Read the sentences.

Mom at Work

1. We like to win.
2. We get help **from** my mom.
3. **She** works with **us**.
4. If we win, we have a **very good day**.

What is a very good day for you?

 **Phonics Games**
NGReach.com

3

My Mother at Work

by Lada Kratky

illustrated by Alessia Girasole

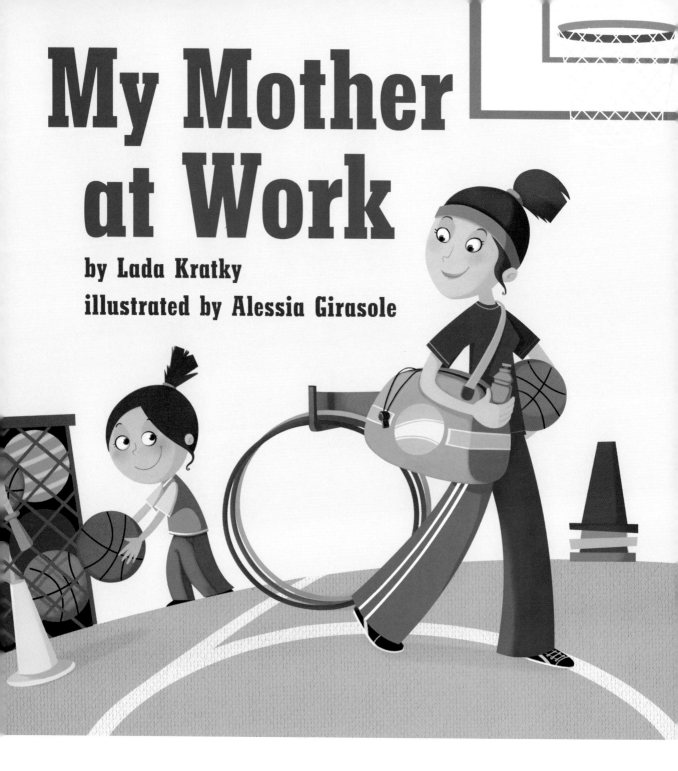

My mom has a job at the gym.

She is very good at it.

She helps us jog.

She helps us hop.

She helps us jab at the bag.

She helps us zig zag.

She helps us win! ❖

Sounds for b, w, j, z

Read these words.

Bob	bag	zig zag	jab	Sam
win	job	jog	Jim	Jan

Find the words that start with **b**.
Then find words with **w**, **j**, and **z**.
Use letters to build them.

b   a   g

Talk Together

Choose words from the box to talk
about what you see in the picture.

Jim can jab.

11

Words with Short <u>e</u>

e

Look at each picture. Read the words.

Example:

h<u>e</u>n

r<u>e</u>d

b<u>e</u>d

l<u>e</u>g

t<u>e</u>n

p<u>e</u>n

High Frequency
Words

day
from
good
she
us
very

Key Words

Read the sentences. Look at the pictures.

We Like Deb

1. Deb is **very good** to **us**.
2. **She** hops **from** Dad to Mom.
3. It is a good **day** if I am with Deb.

What can Deb do?

Phonics Games

NGReach.com

13

Red,
the Hen

by Lada Kratky

illustrated by Hector Borlasca

Red is a hen.

She is a very good hen.

We get an egg a day from Red.

pig pen

We can find an egg in the pig pen.

We can find an egg on the bed.

net

We can find an egg in a net.

Can you find ten eggs from Red? ❖

Words with Short <u>e</u>

Read these words.

wet	jet	pig	big	tan
ten	hen	red	dog	pet

Find the words with short **e**. Use these letters to build the words.

p e t

Talk Together

The <u>hen</u> is <u>red</u>.

Choose words from the box above. Tell your partner what you see in the picture.

A Very Good Day

What do Jen and Jim do on a very good day? Read the sentences. Find the pictures to match. What 2 pictures don't belong?

1. Wes jogs with us.
2. We jab at bags.
3. We zig zag.
4. We get wet.
5. Jen has jam.

Acknowledgments
Grateful acknowledgment is given to the authors, artists, photographers, museums, publishers, and agents for permission to reprint copyrighted material. Every effort has been made to secure the appropriate permission. If any omissions have been made or if corrections are required, please contact the Publisher.

Photographic Credits
CVR (Cover) Eliane Sulle/Alamy Images. **2** (bl) Sergej Razvodovskij/Shutterstock. (br) Ashley Cooper/Alamy Images. (tl) Tereshchenko Dmitry/Shutterstock. (tr) Annette/Shutterstock. **3** (b) Liz Garza Williams/Hampton-Brown/National Geographic School Publishing. **11** (t) Liz Garza Williams/Hampton-Brown/National Geographic School Publishing. **12** (br) SimonovA/ Shutterstock. (cl) Comstock/Getty Images. (cr) Liane Cary/age fotostock. (tl) George Clerk/ iStockphoto. (tr) ryasick photography/Shutterstock. **13** (b) Liz Garza Williams/Hampton-Brown/ National Geographic School Publishing. **21** (t) Liz Garza Williams/Hampton-Brown/National Geographic School Publishing.

Illustrator Credits
3, 11, 13, 21, 22-23 Steve Mack; **4-10** Alessia Girasole; **14-20** Hector Borlasca

The National Geographic Society
John M. Fahey, Jr., President & Chief Executive Officer
Gilbert M. Grosvenor, Chairman of the Board

Copyright © 2011 The Hampton-Brown Company, Inc., a wholly owned subsidiary of the National Geographic Society, publishing under the imprints National Geographic School Publishing and Hampton-Brown.

All rights reserved. No part of this book may be reproduced or transmitted in any form or by any means, electronic or mechanical, including photocopying, recording, or by an information storage and retrieval system, without permission in writing from the Publisher.

National Geographic and the Yellow Border are registered trademarks of the National Geographic Society.

National Geographic School Publishing
Hampton-Brown
www.NGSP.com

Printed in the USA.
Quad Graphics, Leominster, MA

ISBN:978-0-7362-8025-9

17 18 19
10 9 8 7 6